Why do boomerangs come back?

Disney BOOKS BY MAIL

When Mickey Wonders Why, he searches out
the answers with a little
help from these friendly experts:

Vice President and Publisher Cathryn Clark Girard
Director, Product Development Kristina Jorgensen
Editorial Director Lisa Ann Marsoli

DK Direct Limited
Managing Art Editor Eljay Crompton
Senior Editor Rosemary McCormick
Writer Alexandra Parsons
Illustrators The Alvin White Studios and Richard Manning
Designers Amanda Barlow, Wayne Blades, Veneta Bullen,
Richard Clemson, Sarah Goodwin, Diane Klein, Sonia Whillock

Contents

How does a kaleidoscope work?

If you look in a kaleidoscope, you will see a pattern of pretty colored pieces. You seem to see a complete circle. But really it is just a few pieces reflected in mirrors over and over. When you turn the tube, the pattern changes because you are moving the pieces around and so a different design is reflected.

How to make a kaleidoscope
1. Divide a piece of cardboard into three pieces.
2. Stick foil on, shiny side up.
3. Bend card into triangular tube shape, with the foil on the inside.
4. At one end, sandwich colored beads between plastic and white paper.
5. Make a peephole at the other end.

Reflection facts

☞ The kaleidoscope was invented by a Scotsman named Sir David Brewster over a hundred years ago.

☞ The word kaleidoscope comes from a Greek word which means looking at beautiful forms.

5

How does a ventriloquist make a dummy speak?

Well, the dummy doesn't really speak – it just seems as if it does. It's the person holding the dummy who's doing the talking. That person is called a ventriloquist (ven-TRIL-o-quist). Ventriloquists can talk without moving their lips. They breathe deeply and move just the tip of their tongue. They move the dummy's mouth to fool the audience.

Talking hand
Paint a face on the side of your hand, and move your thumb to make the mouth work.

Famous dummy

Charlie McCarthy is one of the most famous dummies in the world. He's even more well known than his ventriloquist partner, Edgar Bergen.

Dummy facts

☞ The two most difficult letters to say without moving your lips, are P and B. Try saying – "brown bread and butter," or "pretty polly parrot."

☞ The word ventriloquist comes from two Latin words – one means belly, the other means to speak.

How do tightrope walkers stay on the tightrope?

Because they keep the center of their body weight balanced directly above the wire. Carrying a pole, or holding their arms outstretched, helps pull their weight down equally on either side of the wire so they don't fall off.

The ear canal
The signals to help us balance come from our ear canals in our inner ear. They are tiny, curly tubes filled with fluid. As we move, the fluid whooshes around tiny ear hairs containing nerve fibers. The fibers send messages to our brain to let us know if we're tipping over.

Balancing potato man

You will need a potato, toothpicks for his legs and arms, two forks and some wire. Make a notch in the bottom of one leg so it will fit on the wire. Stick the forks in either side to make him balance.

Balancing facts

☞ Just like the long pole helps the tightrope walker balance on the wire, the forks help balance the potato man.

☞ A high-wire walker called Henri Rochetain stayed up on a wire for 185 days. He even slept balanced on the wire.

Why do boomerangs come back?

Because of their shape and how they are thrown. A boomerang is shaped like a wing – it has a flat bottom and a curved top. When a boomerang is thrown at a certain angle, this shape helps to lift it into the air and spin it in many circles. It makes so many circles that it comes back to where it started.

Having fun

Boomerangs aren't the only things you can have fun throwing. If you throw something flat and round, it will whiz through the air, too.

Facts that come back

 Australian Aborigines invented the boomerang thousands of years ago. They used boomerangs for different things. Some boomerangs were big, heavy, and almost straight. These were used for hunting and didn't come back. The curved boomerangs were used for sport.

How can you get a ship inside a bottle?

By building it so that it can fold flat. The ship is pushed through the neck of the bottle and glued to a blue-colored clay sea. There are little threads on the masts so they can be pulled up straight from the outside once the ship is in the bottle.

Bottles of fun
What has a neck but cannot swallow?
A bottle!

12

n the bottle

After the ship has been put into he bottle, the masts are pulled p straight. The sails and the eck fittings are stuck on with rops of glue on the end of long, hin wires.

What are shadow puppets?

They are shapes, held between a light and a wall or screen, so that the shapes make shadows. Shadows form where light rays cannot reach. The shapes can be of different things, such as animals and people.

Night light

If you place your hand between a light source and a pale-colored wall or screen you will be ready to make shadow puppets. A small lamp will throw sharp shadows. Larger lamps make softer shadows.

It's magic!

 The Chinese were the first to make puppets for fun. Long, long, ago Chinese emperors were entertained by shadow puppets made from very fancy paper cut-outs.

 Link your thumbs together and point your fingers upward, then flap your hands to make your bird fly.

How do funhouse mirrors work?

Mirrors work by reflecting light rays from our bodies back to our eyes. Regular mirrors reflect our image straight back, so we look normal. But when mirrors are curved the image in the mirror is reflected back at different angles. That's why mirrors that curve outward usually make us look larger and mirrors that curve inward always make us look smaller.

Left or right?
When you look in a mirror, what you see is reversed. Write your name on a piece of paper and hold it up to a mirror. What do you see?

Look at me!

Mirrors are sheets of glass that have a silvery coating on the back. When you look into a mirror, your image is reflected back by the silvery coating, not by the glass.

Spoon face

 Look into the bowl of a spoon – your face will look enormous! Then look at the back of the spoon, your face will look tiny!

How does a magnifying glass work?

The curved glass of the lens bends light rays and spreads them out wider. So when you hold a magnifying glass at a certain angle, and look through it, you see things spread out and much bigger.

Seeing up close
A microscope allows us to see things that are too small to see with our eyes alone. It has lots of magnifying lenses stacked on top of each other to make the image look much bigger.

Seeing into the distance
Telescopes let you see far, far into the distance. They have big curved lenses like dishes. These dishes collect light rays from far away, turning tiny specks in the sky into great big close-ups.

I see!

☞ A modern microscope can make something look thousands of times bigger than it is.

☞ Nearly 400 years ago, the Italian scientist, Galileo, was the first person to use a telescope to look at the sky.

How do you make bottles sing?

By blowing air across the top of them. The air you blow inside the bottle moves very quickly – or vibrates – and makes a sound. The less air there is in the bottle, the higher the note. An empty bottle makes the deepest sound, so as you fill the bottle with water, the note becomes higher.

20

Fizzy fun
What would you call six
bottles of soda?
A pop group!

Name that tune!

☞ When you get tired blowing into the bottles, you can turn them into a xylophone just by hitting the bottles with a stick.

☞ You can also make a musical instrument by placing a piece of paper around the teeth of a comb, and then blow air through the paper.

Twing twang!

Would you like to make your own guitar? You will need a shoebox and some rubber bands of different sizes. Cut a hole in the lid of the box, then stretch the rubber bands around it.

Why do some balloons float up and away?

Balloons filled with ordinary air just bounce and sink to the ground. But balloons filled with a special gas called helium will float up high into the sky – unless you hold on to the string. That's because helium is lighter than air.

Amazing airships
The first passenger "aircraft" were held up by a bag filled with a light gas called hydrogen. They were called airships. People were carried in cabins underneath called gondolas.

Up, up and away

👉 Two Frenchmen named Joseph and Jacques Montgolfier built the first hot air balloon that could carry people into the air. It made its first flight in Paris, France, on November 21, 1783. That was over 100 years before the first airplane flight.

How do fireworks work?

Fireworks have a long strip of paper, gunpowder, and colored chemicals inside. The strip of paper is called a fuse. When the fuse is lit it sets fire to the gunpowder and the gunpowder sets fire to the colored chemicals. The chemicals burst and make the pretty lights we see as the gunpowder throws them up into the air.

Where did it all begin?

The Chinese invented gunpowder and then invented fireworks. On Chinese New Year, people like to celebrate with lots of noisy firecrackers.

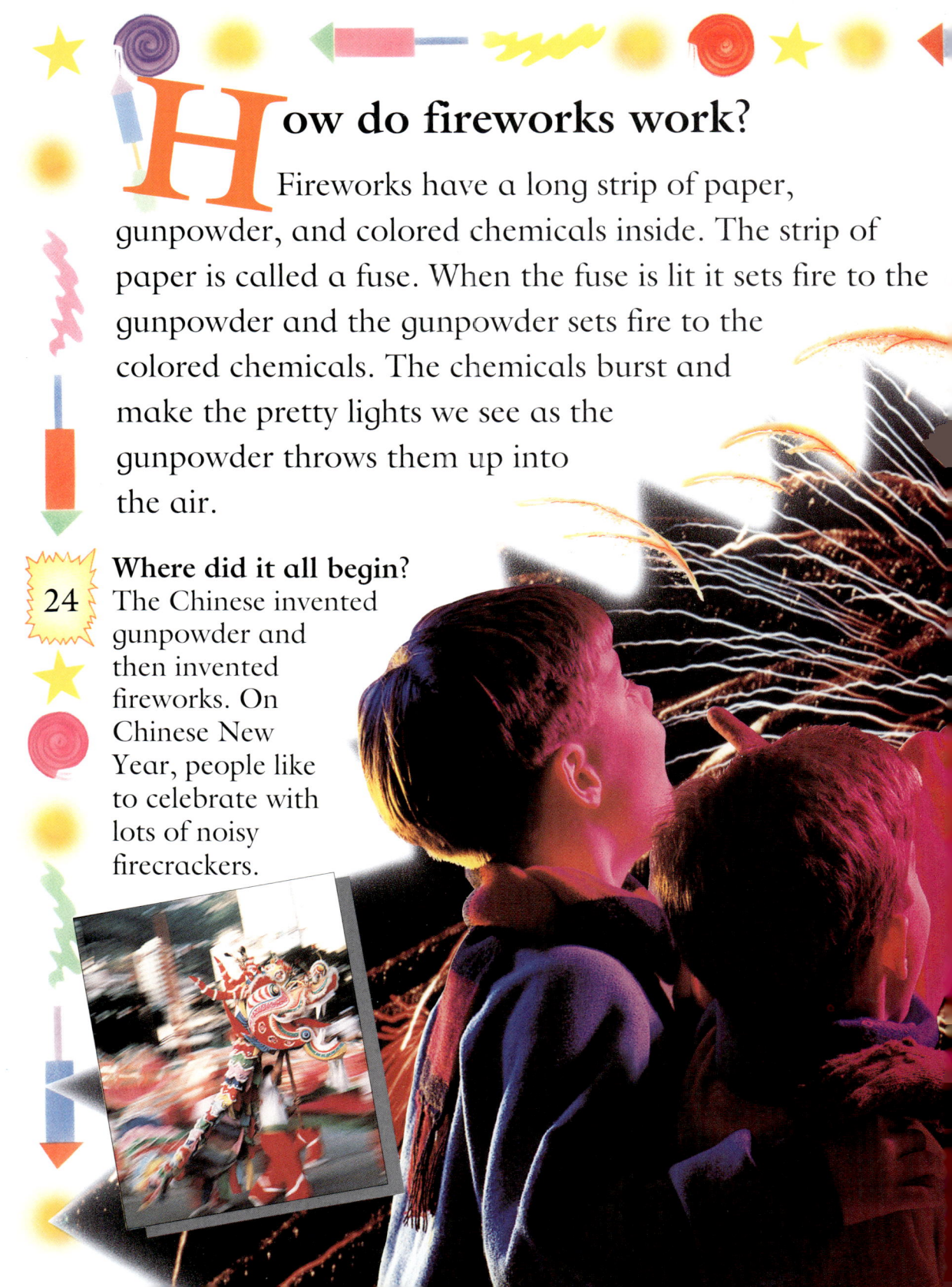

Explosive fireworks facts

👉 Fireworks look beautiful but they can be VERY DANGEROUS. That's why only specially trained people are in charge of fireworks displays.

👉 Distress flares are fireworks used by ships that are in trouble at sea. Ships send up red flares so other ships and planes in the area know they need help.

25

What are mazes?

They are pathways which are supposed to confus[e] and puzzle you – especially when you're looking for the way out! Many mazes are made out of hedges. People in Europe used to put them in their gardens because they looked nice, and also entertained their guests.

Which way?
America's most famous hedge maze is in the gardens of the Governor's Palace at Williamsburg, Virginia.

Having fun
Some people love mazes so much, they have built wooden ones to have lots of fun in!

Walls of fun
What did one wall say to the other wall?
I'll meet you at the corner!

A-maze-ing facts

👉 Mazes were probably the first puzzles. Maze patterns have been found carved into rocks and caves all over the world.

👉 In Casa Grande, Arizona, there are maze carvings on rocks which date back to the 1200s.

MICKEY'S Mind teaser

Mickey would like you to come to his party. Just follow the balloons to find your way through the maze.